To all of my students from S⟨...⟩
and beyond. You are in ⟨...⟩
of your own future, make th⟨...⟩
Mr. Rich

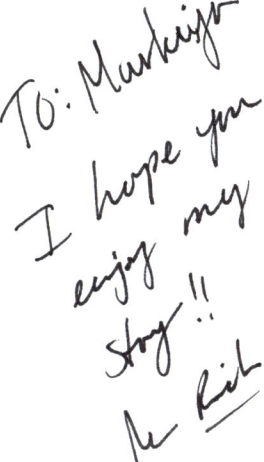

TO: Markiys
I hope you
enjoy my
story!!
Mr. Rich

Saturday
Text © 2014 – Tyrone Richardson
Illustrations © 2014 - Casey Dilzer
(Water color and ink)
Printed in United States of America (USA)
Published by Teach One Publishing
http://www.TeachOnePublishing.com
All rights reserved.

ISBN 978-1-62847-322-3

Monday I can't think,

always the same.

I get to school late,

siblings to blame.

Didn't have breakfast,

can't stand this class.

I get yelled at,

everyone laughs.

On the block later,

I like to hang.

You probably guessed it,

down with a gang.

Well no, not really,

not anyway yet.

When I get home

my mother says,

"On Saturday you're going

to see your father!"

Tuesday I can't think,

always the same.

Still get to school late,

siblings to blame.

Didn't have breakfast,

can't stand this class.

Same clothes as yesterday,

everyone laughs.

I got it bad sometimes,

in trouble in school a lot.

Dad quit school,

he chilled on the block.

On Wednesday they meet

to find out what to do.

To help my grades go up

and get me through school.

It's not like I don't know,

sometimes I don't care...

to answer the square root of 25,

or who, what, when,

why, or where.

Thursday is a half day,

that means no school for me.

We get to eat breakfast today,

and on top of that watch TV.

Who's your baby's daddy,

who's cheatin on who?

This is way more interesting

then what we learn in school!!

"Mmmhmm..just like your daddy, with his good for nothing behind!!! I got some words for him on Saturday!!"

She got some words for him
makes me start to think.
What do I have to
say to my Dad?

I wonder if his other kids visit.

I wonder if he's sad.

I get crazy confused today wondering about my dad.

Friday I can't think,

always the same.

I get to school late,

siblings to blame.

Didn't have breakfast,

can't stand this class.

I can't hear anyone,

don't care if they laugh.

My whole day is focused

on words for my Dad.

So I block out everything

from the first word to the last.

> Why didn't you finish school?
> Why are you in here?
> Do you still love my mom?
> Do you even care?
> When are you getting out?
> What will you do?
> Is it cool to be in here?
> Should I look up to you?

The words just flowed on and on, question after question.
On Friday night I could hardly sleep, awaiting our session.

Saturday came and it was time

to go and visit Dad...

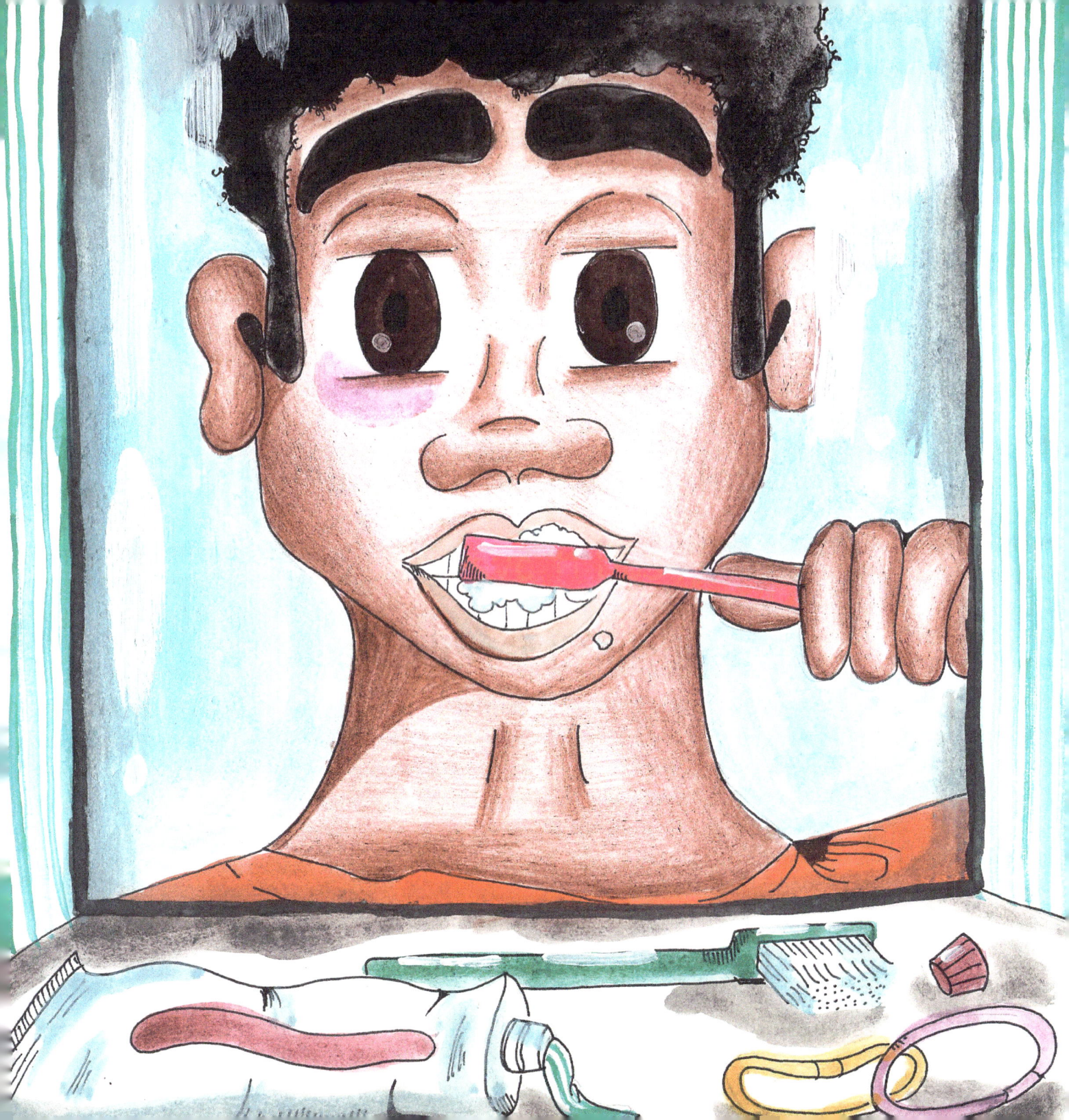

I got in the car with my list and read it over and over again until I fell asleep.

When I woke up we were there,
State Prison.

So what's next? It can't possibly end like this! You decide. What will our main character say to his father? Will he use the list? What will his dad say? Will they be happy to see each other? What do you think will happen next? Write your your own ending.

_____
_____
_____
_____
_____
_____
_____
_____
_____
_____

CPSIA information can be obtained at www.ICGtesting.com
Printed in the USA
BVOW11s0332031014
369359BV00002B/3/P

9 781628 473223